When Whales CROSS the SEA

THE GREY WHALE MIGRATION

by Sharon Katz Cooper

illustrated by Tom Leonard

raintree
a Capstone company — publishers for children

Raintree is an imprint of Capstone Global Library Limited, a company incorporated in England and Wales having its registered office at 7 Pilgrim Street, London, EC4V 6LB – Registered company number: 6695582

www.raintree.co.uk
myorders@raintree.co.uk

With thanks to our advisers for their expertise, research and advice:

Diane Alps, Marine Mammal Biologist
Cabrillo Marine Aquarium, San Pedro, California, USA

Terry Flaherty, PhD, Professor of English
Minnesota State University, Mankato, USA

Editorial Credits
Jill Kalz, editor; Lori Bye, designer; Nathan Gassman, art director; Laura Manthe, production specialist

ISBN 978 1 4747 6468 1
21..20..19..18 17
10 9 8 7 6 5 4 3 2 1

British Library Cataloguing in Publication Data
A full catalogue record for this book is available from the British Library.

Photo Credits
The illustrations in this book were created with acrylics.
Image Credit: XNR Productions, 3 (map)

Printed and bound in India.

Every year, grey whales make one of the longest migrations of any mammal on Earth. They swim 8,000 to 11,000 kilometres (5,000 to 7,000 miles) from their summer homes to warm winter waters. Swimming nearly 160 kilometres (100 miles) per day, they complete the journey in two to three months. Why do they travel so far?

RUSSIA

ARCTIC OCEAN

Alaska

0   300   600 miles
0   300   600 kilometres

N
W   E
S

CANADA

PACIFIC OCEAN

UNITED STATES

ATLANTIC OCEAN

MEXICO

- - - - - grey whale migration route

Swish! ... BUMP! The whale hits the edge of a large ice chunk. She's done that three times already this week.

It is October in the Arctic, and patches of ice are getting larger. Days are getting shorter. Waters are getting colder. Feeding season is almost over. The whale knows it's time to start heading south, to the warmer waters of Mexico. She has something very important to do there.

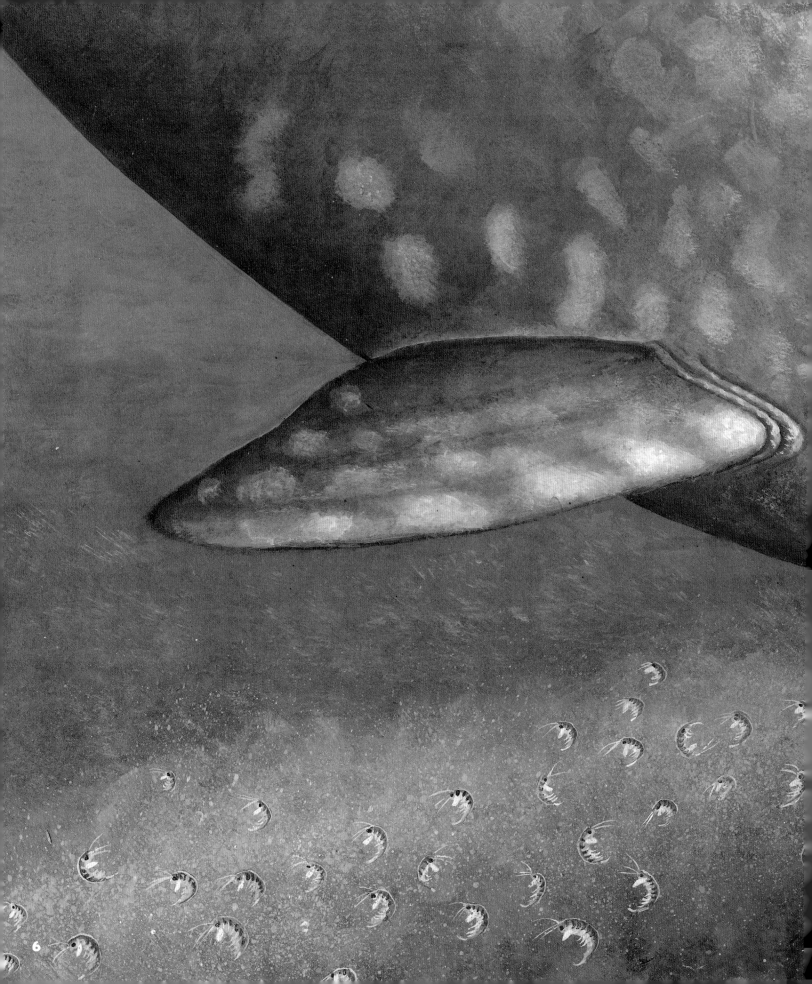

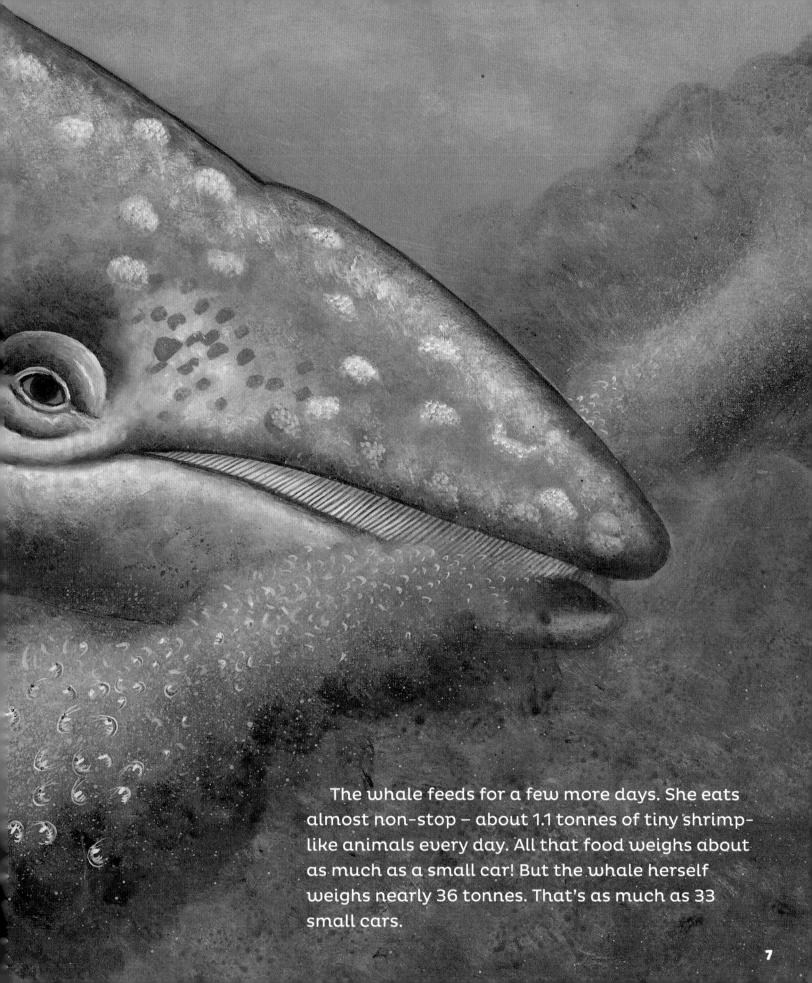

The whale feeds for a few more days. She eats almost non-stop – about 1.1 tonnes of tiny shrimp-like animals every day. All that food weighs about as much as a small car! But the whale herself weighs nearly 36 tonnes. That's as much as 33 small cars.

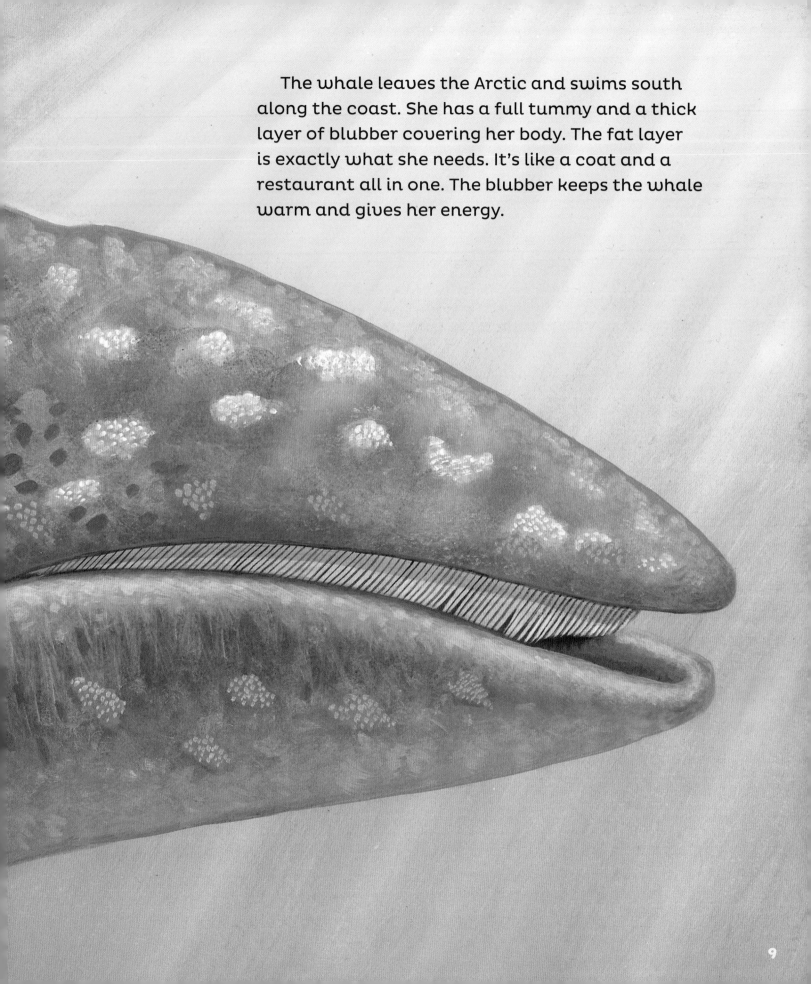

The whale leaves the Arctic and swims south along the coast. She has a full tummy and a thick layer of blubber covering her body. The fat layer is exactly what she needs. It's like a coat and a restaurant all in one. The blubber keeps the whale warm and gives her energy.

The whale swims with power through the sea. She stays close to the shore, where the water is shallower. Shallow water means less chance of meeting a hungry orca.

She peeks her head above water. Landmarks on the shore help her to find her way.

During the journey the whale slows down to rest, but she never stops. She doesn't even eat. She must get to her winter home on time. A warm coastal lagoon awaits her. There is no time to waste.

Finally, after about 60 days, the whale's journey ends – just in time too! She's having a baby! A healthy, 454-kilogram (1,000-pound) baby whale.

The baby whale must grow quickly. In a few months, he will join his mother for the long journey back northwards. He does not have a thick layer of blubber yet. The waters of the lagoon keep him warm while he is still small.

The lagoon is safe from orcas. But it doesn't have a lot of food. To help him grow, the mother whale feeds her baby 189 litres (50 gallons) of milk every day. He can gain up to 27 kilograms (60 pounds) each day! At the same time, the mother whale loses a lot of blubber. She does not eat much and puts her energy into making milk.

The mother whale helps her baby to swim. She shows him how to plough up the seabed to look for food. He will need to do this when they reach their summer home in the Arctic.

After three months it is time to start the long, challenging trip northwards. There are many dangers on this journey, including orcas, large ships and polluted waters.

Good luck on your journey, whales. Be safe, and see you next year!

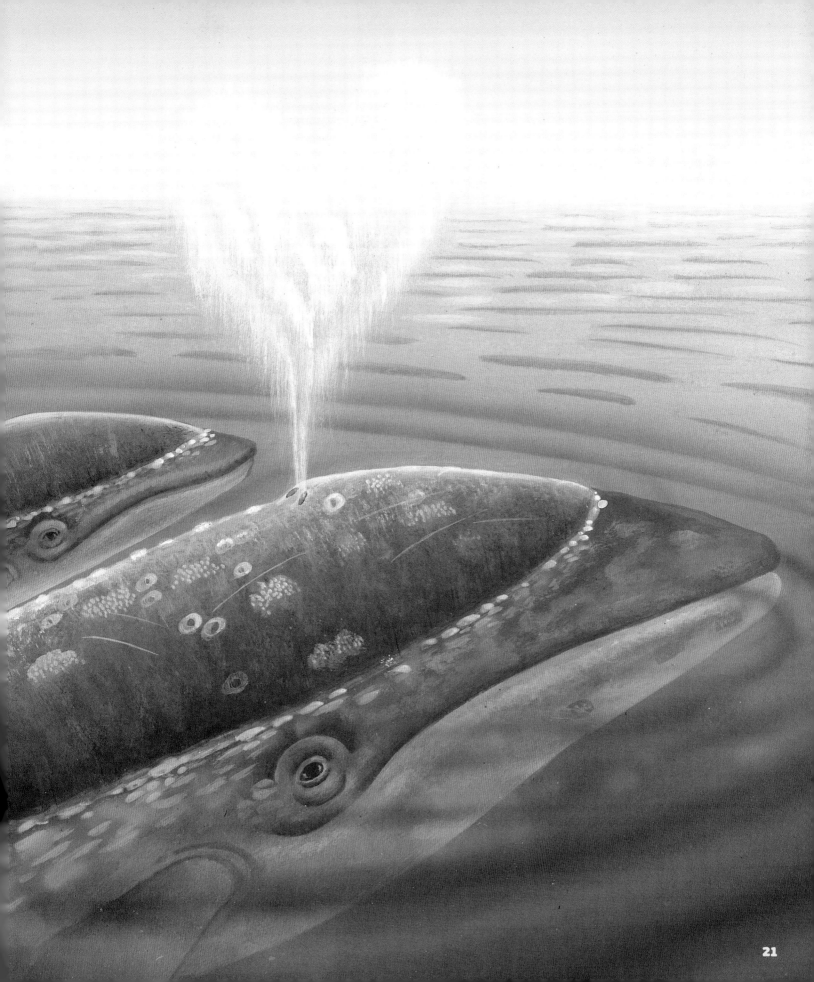

Grey Whale Fast Facts

Scientific name: *Eschrichtius robustus*

Type of whale: baleen (filters food through a comb-like structure called baleen, rather than using teeth)

Adult weight: 36–41 tonnes

Weight at birth: 454–680 kilograms (1,000–1,500 pounds)

Whale milk: very thick and rich; 53 per cent fat (human milk is about 2 per cent fat)

Nursing: young whales drink their mother's milk for 7 to 9 months

Diet: amphipods and tube worms from the seabed; grey whales are the only whales that feed in this way

Blubber layer: 15–25 centimetres (6–10 inches)

Life span: 60 years or more

Predators: orcas and humans

Total length of migration: 16,100 to 22,500 kilometres (10,000 to 14,000 miles) in total per migration

Comprehension Questions

1. Why can't grey whales stay in the waters of the Arctic Ocean all year? Why do they migrate south?

2. Describe how the mother whale takes care of her baby in the lagoon.

3. Look at the map on page 3. What does the dotted line show?

Glossary

amphipod small shrimp-like animal

blubber thick layer of fat under the skin of some animals

coastal lagoon large, shallow body of water protected from the sea by barrier islands

landmark something that stands out, such as a big tree or a building

mammal warm-blooded animal that breathes air; mammals have hair or fur; female mammals give birth to live young and feed them milk

migration movement from one area to another on a regular basis, usually to find food or to produce young

orca also known as a killer whale; the orca is a black and white whale, it is the ocean's top predator

polluted dirty and harmful to living things

predator animal that hunts other animals

Read More

Animal Infographics (Infographics), Chris Oxlade (Raintree, 2014)

Ocean Food Chains (Food Chains and Webs), Angela Royston (Raintree, 2012)

Whales (Great Migrations), Laura Marsh (National Geographic Society, 2010)

Websites

www.bbc.co.uk/nature/life/Gray_Whale
Learn more about grey whales, and watch some amazing videos on the BBC website.

www.kids.nationalgeographic.com
Visit the Kids National Geographic website and search for all the latest news on animal migration.

www.whaleroute.com
Discover more amazing facts about grey whales and look in more detail at maps of whale migratory patterns.

Index

LOOK OUT FOR ALL THE BOOKS IN THE SERIES:

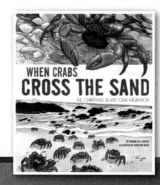

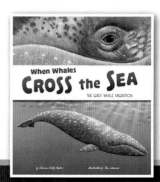